Abadaba Alphabet
Learning Letter Sounds

by Sheila Moore

pictures by Carol Holsinger

Abadaba Alphabet

Text Copyright © 2006 by Sheila Moore   Illustrations Copyright © 2006 by Carol Holsinger

First Edition

With appreciation for their help and advice to Ellen Braaf, Val Hope, John Morton,
Linda Sittig, Pam Taggart, Beckie Weinheimer, and Danielle Welch. Most of all, deepest thanks
to my daughter, Carol, and my husband, Harry, for their unfailing support.

And with special tribute to the exceptional achievements of Steven Langston Mitchell.

ISBN-13: 978-0-9789473-0-9
ISBN-10: 0-9789473-0-4
Library of Congress Control Number: 2006908113

Published by Abadaba Reading LLC, P.O. Box 80, Charlottesville, VA 22902

Printed in the United States of America

To my grandchildren,

Ben, Campbell, Josh, Malcolm, and Virginia Rose

Abadaba alphabet,

appaloosaloo,

see a letter, sound a letter,

a ✦✦✦ a ✦✦✦ a

apples, ants and astrocats,

alligator acrobats.

(say the "a" in a-pples)

Abadaba alphabet,

butterfingeroo,

see a letter, sound a letter,

b☆☆b☆☆b

bobcat, bike and baby bears,

blue baboons in beanbag chairs.

(say the "b" in b-ike)

Abadaba alphabet,
    crackajackeroo,
see a letter, sound a letter,

C ★ C ★ C

    cupcakes, crickets, cockatoos,
cows in cantaloupe canoes.

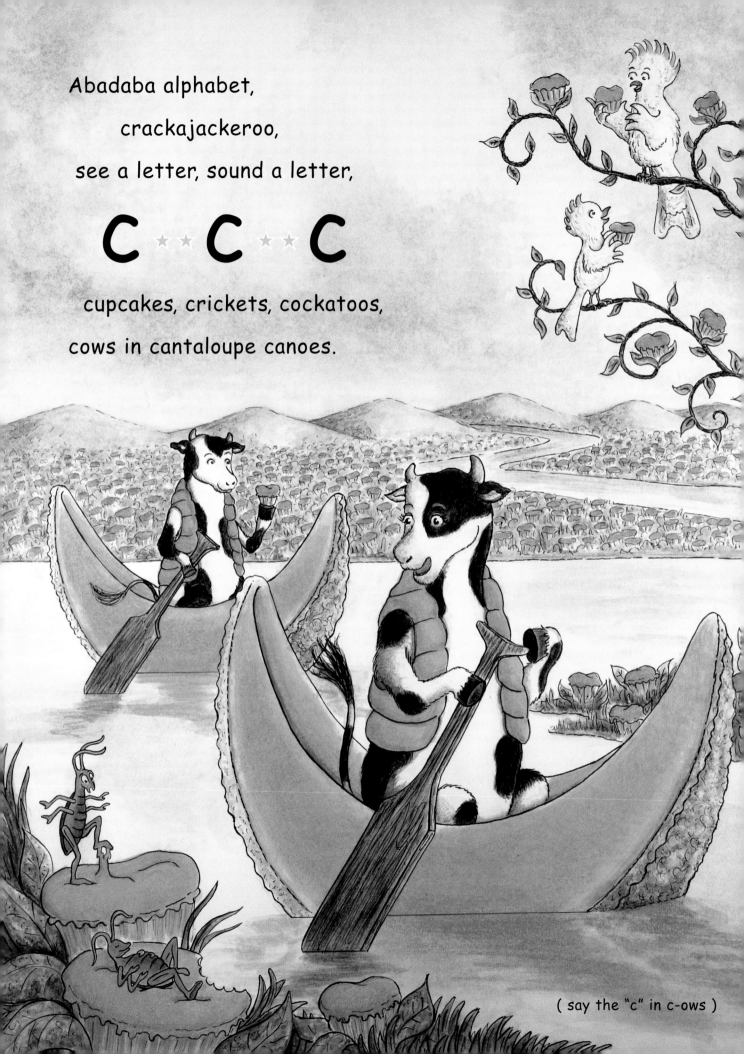

(say the "c" in c-ows)

Abadaba alphabet,
dipsydoodledoo,
see a letter, sound a letter,

d ✦ d ✦ d

dentist, duckling, dominoes,
dapper dogs dance do-si-dos.

(say the "d" in d-ogs)

Abadaba alphabet,

enchiladaloo,

see a letter, sound a letter,

e ⋆ e ⋆ e

eggs and echo, evergreens,

elephants in emerald jeans.

(say the "e" in e-ggs)

Abadaba alphabet,

fiddlefaddlefoo,

see a letter, sound a letter,

f☆☆f☆☆f

fun and feathers, fish and flutes,

ferrets flip in frogman suits.

(say the "f" in f-un)

Abadaba alphabet,

giddyuparoo,

see a letter, sound a letter,

g ☆ g ☆ g

gliders, goggles, go-kart wheels,

geese and goats play glockenspiels.

(say the "g" in g-oats)

Abadaba alphabet,
  hunkydorydoo,
  see a letter, sound a letter,
  h✰✰h✰✰h
    hammers, hubcaps, hens and hogs,
  hippos high-step wearing clogs.

(say the "h" in h-ens)

Abadaba alphabet,

  itsybitsyboo,

see a letter, sound a letter,

i ☆☆ i ☆☆ i

  iguana, insects, it and if,

itchy inchworms climb a cliff.

(say the "i" in i-f)

Abadaba alphabet,

    jackadandydoo,

see a letter, sound a letter,

J ☆☆ J ☆☆ J

jingle, jogger, jazz and jeans,

jackals jump for jellybeans.

(say the "j" in j-azz)

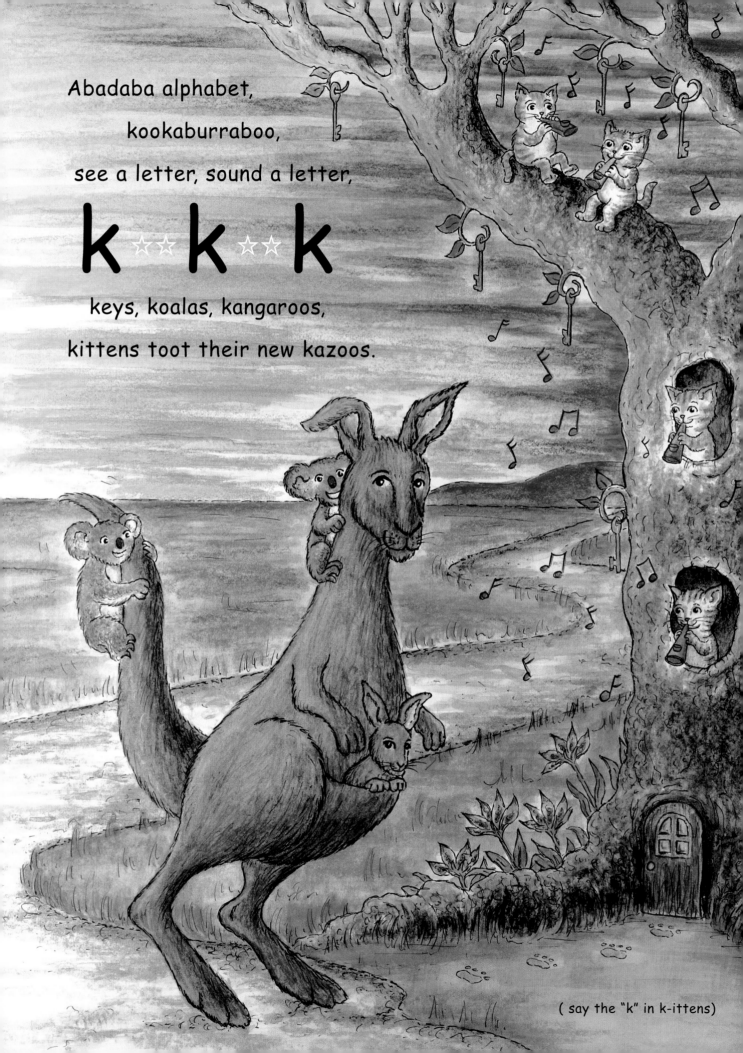

Abadaba alphabet,
    kookaburraboo,
see a letter, sound a letter,

k☆k☆k

    keys, koalas, kangaroos,
kittens toot their new kazoos.

(say the "k" in k-ittens)

Abadaba alphabet,

lollipopaloo,

see a letter, sound a letter,

I ☆ ☆ **I** ☆ ☆ **I**

lion, lemons, lunch and locks,

ladybugs in lilac socks.

(say the "l" in l-ion)

Abadaba alphabet,
    mozzarellaroo,
    see a letter, sound a letter,

m ✦ m ✦ m

    music, mice and mandolin,
    monkey takes his medicine.

(say the "m" in m-ice)

Abadaba alphabet,

   nittygrittygoo,

see a letter, sound a letter,

n☆☆n☆☆n

napkin, necklace, newts and nine,

nosy nighthawks come to dine.

(say the "n" in n-ine)

Abadaba alphabet,
olleytrolleytoo,
see a letter, sound a letter,

O ☆☆ O ☆☆ O

otter, ox, and ocelot,
ostrich on an olive yacht.

(say the "o" in o-tter)

Abadaba alphabet,
pumpernickeloo,
see a letter, sound a letter,

p ☆ p ☆ p

playpen, pillow, pears and pies,
poodle pups with purple ties.

(say the "p" in p-ups)

Abadaba alphabet,
   quibbledibbledoo,
   see a letter, sound a letter,

q ☆☆ q ☆☆ q

   quilts and question, queens that quack,
   quail cheer on the quarterback.

(say the "qu" [kw] in qu-ack)

Abadaba alphabet,

   razzledazzleloo,

  see a letter, sound a letter,

r ☆ r ☆ r

  rainbow, runner, rabbits, ring,

  rams and reindeer rock and sing.

(say the "r" in r-ing)

Abadaba alphabet,

superduperoo,

see a letter, sound a letter,

S☆☆S☆☆S

see-saw, scissors, snow and snakes,

seven skunks with stomach aches.

(say the "s" in s-nakes)

Abadaba alphabet,
　　teenybopperoo,
see a letter, sound a letter,

✝ ☆☆ ✝ ☆☆ ✝

teepee, turtle, toy and train,
　　tigers taxi in the rain.

(say the "t" in t-oy)

Abadaba alphabet,
   upsydaisydoo,
   see a letter, sound a letter,

u ☆☆ u ☆☆ u

   uncles rest in ugly chairs,
   umbrella birds unpack upstairs.

(say the "u" in u-npack)

Abadaba alphabet,

  vermicellivoo,

  see a letter, sound a letter,

V ☆ V ☆ V

  van, volcano, velvet bows,

  vultures viewing videos.

(say the "v" in v-an)

Abadaba alphabet,

wibblewobblewoo,

see a letter, sound a letter,

W✫✫W✫✫W

wagon, whippet, waffles, woof,

weasels waltzing on the roof.

(say the "w" in w-agon)

Abadaba alphabet,
   pixiedixiedoo,
see a letter, sound a letter,

X ☆☆ X ☆☆ X

tux and mixer, box and wax,
   six red foxes model slacks.

(say the "x" [ks] in wa-x)

Abadaba alphabet,

yankeedoodleloo,

see a letter, sound a letter,

Y☆Y☆Y

yellow yo-yos, yummy hats,

yaks atop their yoga mats.

(say the "y" in y-ak)

Abadaba alphabet,
   zippadeezeedoo,
see a letter, sound a letter,

Z ☆☆ Z ☆☆ Z

   zeros, zigzag, zipper, zoo,
zebras love zucchini stew.

(say the "z" in z-oo)

Abadaba alphabet,
   sound and see and say,
apples all the way to zoo,
   hey, hey, heigh-ho, hurray!

The End